Whatever It Takes to Make Us Feel Alive

Bill Edmondson

FUTURECYCLE PRESS
www.futurecycle.org

Published by FutureCycle Press
Hayesville, North Carolina, USA

ISBN 978-1-938853-23-4

Contents

For Walker and Casey

"...whatever it takes to make us feel alive."

—from early review of "Vertigo"

I

Harpo's Monkey

Understand
How much fun the monkey is   how warm and playful
Yet one day
He smothers it   drives out to Riverbend
Throws it in
When he gets home   scratches stinging along his arms
It's in the bedroom mewling out its hunger
He feeds his sweet monkey
Smiles as he watches it eat

Understand
The secret they share is beautiful
He and his flamboyant monkey
They know the intense pleasure in willed weakness
The paradise locked in strangers   they know
The silky texture of the master key   still
He shoots the monkey   throws it
Into a dumpster out on Canal Street   On his way home
There it is with its thumb out   *He'll speed on by*
Stops   lets in his monkey

What's he gonna do with such a monkey?
He waits until it's in their tiled bathroom
Lops off its head that dances in the tub
Mails the dismembered sections UPS   Later   exhausted
Goes to the Avenue Pub
Where the small man on the next stool
Turns toward him and is of course the monkey

Using its man's voice it asks
Where're we goin' tonight?

A Question

1

Why   on a day like any other in his car
singing along with Alabama
those words about discovery—
about your firstborn held against your chest the first time—
after losing the local Country station as the hills rose
          behind him
switching to National Public Radio where he heard
                    child abuse is up
and found with another mild curse he'd forgotten his watch again
and with no clock in his old car he'd have to rely on displays
on banks and auto dealerships: 1:05
1:15   1:33   traffic only moderate
greening hills painting out winter and then
coming down out of the rainbow tunnel   banking right and left
approaching the dizzying scale of the Golden Gate Bridge
beyond it the city where he'd dreamed and still worked
          and nearing 2 p.m.
had yet plenty of time to prepare
          for his classes
and after those bridge scenes always the same: a tourist family
grouped for a photo: joggers   lovers   a father holding his child
          under his gray jacket
only pajamaed feet hanging past daddy's belt
and after the adrenaline shot because he'd looked too long
          and almost hit another car
glancing back to see a man (the same one?)
receding   walking south   gray jacket open
arms at his sides   veer toward the rail

Why after sleeping in the teacher's lounge
through time he might have used
then raging through his classes for no apparent reason
then driving the freeway wire north in the cold night   home

and after pulling up the kicked-off blankets and kissing his
        sleeping son
why does he stumble past his wife asleep on the sofa
to catch the TV headlines
TODAY   SHORTLY BEFORE TWO P.M. ON THE GOLDEN GATE
    BRIDGE...?

2

Always in daydreams he's a better man   stops on that bridge
is out of his car   leaping all lanes of traffic
sprints along the cement walkway
ignores the adult who brandishes the child
flies straight toward and springs and holds
those red-pajamaed legs

Sometimes he wonders: Why did her father take her?
He might have safely locked her in the car
Someone would have found her
Someone would have loved her in this world

22nd & Collingwood

—for Ednah Helen Tagle

All those nights he stands watch at the rail
Where the two streets meet
Peacoat collar up against the cut of the wind
Against fog behind him spilling down Twin Peaks

Six months off the farm   seventeen   he waits
And you don't show   or show up late
Bright-colored   high on other men
Sweet nectar of *Hypnotique* to get him buzzing—
Remember that first kiss? He had to touch you twice
Before you wrapped around him—

A shipmate tries to warn him off
Draws a cartoon:
Slit-skirt *caliente* on pedestal

You leave the door unlocked at 3 a.m.
Let him into your family home
White hat and shoes left on the porch
He inches up to your bedroom

You know your father hates all sailors
And you remember why:
You were twelve the day it ended
He   remembering Guadalajara festivals
Told you to put on a pretty dress

In a museum   now   a giant photograph
Market Street on VJ Day
A sea of circling white hats
What we can't see:
Puke-slick street   broken glass   booze

Women thrust up in doorways   down in alleys
Their torn clothes

A father frantic against all hands
To shield his preteen daughter
Your kindled face

The Cost of Health Care

—in memory of Cliff Reid

He died eight days ago when his heart exploded
Just before she saw his forehead
Slam the steering wheel
Before she felt the pickup drift and stop
Still in the driveway
Couldn't pull him down out of the cab
Couldn't lend breath to her gray old friend
After half an hour   an ambulance

Now   in a hospital room
He hangs above a bed   curing
Hangs grotesque and sideways in wires and tubes
If not carcass   say mobile
Say wind chimes of bamboo bones
Waiting for a breath
To set them ticking

The doctor you want to kill   knows
The family knows   yet will not know
And the meter runs on through the days

Sweet   biblical   women moisten his lips
Brush hair from his eyes
Have I said they're open?
Have I said his color's great?

On the ninth day   he's disconnected
Laid on his back
As color once again drains gray
Breath slows   stops

Soon   she'll stand in her kitchen
Crack open the distended envelope

The bill unfurls across the floor
Thirty-thousand dollars   itemized
She begins to read them off
All you'll remember is baby powder

Legacy

It's World War II   Vietnam   Afghanistan
A son returns home
There's a house shaped like a barn   painted red
An upstairs bedroom window
It's late spring   warm
A sloping fallow field lit up in daisies   butterflies
A small dog yipping and leaping
It's a son returned   upstairs window   rifle

News From Afghanistan

A single young redwood—
One green soldier in an army
That occupies a hillside—
Is aflame   is defined by flame
This in February   no lightning   no rain
A cataract of mist obscures the dream

Dad's shaping a bow for his crossbow man
The shop door opens   he sees his wife's eyes
Hits the switch and it all winds down

Vertigo: **Whatever It Takes to Make Us Feel Alive**

On the southern approach to the famous bridge
You pass the wheel of the rental to your broken self
Slip down the embankment to old Fort Point
Where Madeleine plucks at   tosses the bouquet
As she leans toward her plunge   you start
As you always will to stop her
Are checked by the shoulder strap   Marjorie   your wife—
Who only wants to see you happy   but you're so strange—
Asks   *Are you okay?*

At Hotel Vertigo on Sutter Street
You pay a clerk to let you stand in Judy's room
Where you spin slowly   arms held in empty embrace

Marjorie's rival   a whipped confection of honey and drug
Not only never existed   she didn't exist in the film

But on the last day of your vacation
After you've driven down Lombard's tourist curves
You feel   nothing
Until   across the intersection
The street dips at an angle you recall
And you're alone in your '56 DeSoto
Trees and bushes not yet planted
All's bright and clean
Below   Madeleine's light green Jaguar slows
At the end of the block   she swings in left
Stops at your red door

Local Lore

At the intersection
Of State 199 and the county road
In a triangle patch of weeds in front of their restaurant
The Lednick's teenage son
Long in love with the tethered goat
Chooses Saturday afternoon
For consummation   causing
Traffic to swerve and stop   children's faces to be turned away
As drivers run to interrupt

So great is his devotion
The enraptured boy holds on

After a month of passing curiosity
Business picks up   The boy is gone
But mom and pop   fraternal twins   do well
Serving smudged sandwiches   tepid soup
Ice-cold Cabernet

Ashes

1

For the time   I'll set aside
Your unspeakable act   Today
In this heat   in the sweep of
Our last natural river
We will as I have often dreamed
Be brothers   Come down to the water
With me   At that cold   hard pour
Between two boulders
We'll put him back

Dropping along the shattered granite trail
My hold on this cardboard box
Heavy as ingot   is absolute   It takes my hand
Pulls me out of balance

Kneel here in the wet river sand   cool
As a compress   Open the box   Cut open
The plastic sack   On the opposite bank
An innocent family picnics

Do I have something to say?

This: He was a good father and a good
Man   As near as I know
Whatever faith he had
He kept

In my dream
He stood on this same river
I've seen him fish a hundred times
Then silently laid down his rod
Took off his hat and
Without looking back—still holding it—
Jumped in   I started forward
Then woke

2

The ceremony eats my strength
Drinks I've drunk come on
All's bright   heightened
Greens and blue   the diamond glint
of sunlight scattered across surface
I see my car high up on Howland Road
It glows   a coal

Even you can't know the reasons
You sledged our friendship of over forty years
Can only say you were   *attracted*
Brother   old friend   bastard rat
It just won't wash

Who Knew?

Back then   at seventeen
Newly loosed on the city
You were Singapore slings   stingers   half-chicken dinners
Rooftop love songs slung into the dark
In Tenderloin bars   older women stared into their drinks
As you crafted ways to stretch your sailor's pay
To buy them more
One took you home for the price of a pint of whiskey
One let you climb through her window
One had you up for tea
Held you in chains

An afternoon on a foggy Sunset avenue:
Children at play
A four-year-old on a tricycle pedals toward you

She's been your wife forty years

White Dresses: Three Kinds of Darkness

1

Lenora sees Jesus
That's it for her husband Al
Who continues to plow the farm
While she   in a bleached nurse's uniform
Witnesses to cows for forty years
One winter   she slips into a pasture
Drifts to her knees in the snow   disappears

2

In that old weeper   Jennifer Jones is Singleton
Whose mind smashes on the rocks
Thought restored   she kneels in the garden
Picks berries for her savior husband's breakfast
When they smear
She holds out glistening fingers
Claws them across her white dress

3

In the front room of a house in San Diego
Kept dark on a sluggish afternoon
Three sailors share a case of Schlitz
Get the fuck out, one of them orders his wife
No   leave her here
From time to time   commanded
A small white dress
Moves from man to man

Incident on the St. Charles Line

As we applaud the a cappella harmony on the streetcar
there's a double jolt   The car's stopped   I see the driver
beating at the glass up front   The door opens and he veers
into the night   Nobody knows   *There's a man underneath*
A woman puts her hand to her mouth says *I'm not going out there*
but we do   I admit I think body parts   Then a silky green dress
off-duty nurse   skids to her knees in the gravel along the track
holding his head   still attached   says *Speak to me right now!*
He doesn't   She says *There's a lot of blood but his pulse is strong*
Red lights cluster and we're cleared to the sidewalk   A guy asks
Does this mean we have to walk?   Someone explains the device
that stopped the car and the scoop that keeps you from the
wheels   Then the EMTs are there with their gurney   Shears
slice up a pant leg   An image of the nurse as she kneels—
dress in the wind's impulse up to her waist—that moment
all decent men look away

Family Cemetery

A clash of galaxies
Send their light through the black of the brain
Of a man standing among bones and dust
In a weedy field   eastern Arkansas

Many of these   the dead in Christ
Wait here to rise to meet him in the air
While the words on the sign on the church
Under the rusting star
Read: "Jesus Coming Soon"

This visitor   curious
Dreams of a fabulous craft
To break through space and time
To knock about   see if anything's home

     After class one day   his student   an old man
     Showed him a photograph
     Of a proud young pilot in the Chinese air force
     But they'd taken his wings   assigned him a wheelbarrow
     For decades he'd pushed it full of stone
     Along the base of the crumbling Wall

All flight is fantasy
And the teacher knows how little he knows
Can only guess that these who peered through smoke
Danced with shine
Had only the turmoil they lived
Then the box and dirt shoveled down
That their name—his name—
Smoothed by wind and rain
Is at last   wind and rain.

...The Most Wonderful Smile in Sonoma County

You leave Safeway
With a carton of frozen words
Don't see her today   the schoolgirl bagging groceries
As she was last week when you   caught by her smile
Drank its humor and flavor
Now   you're sure you've lost her and there's weather
But she's there in the lot collecting carts
Wearing a raincoat with a red *S* on the back
                                   a clear plastic rain hat
She comes near and you're once again a schoolboy
Pouring your simple compliment—
As you do   sense absurdity and danger—
You're very kind   she says

While teaching middle school   a friend of a friend
Was found kissing a student
For this: fired on the spot   brought to trial
Convicted   sent to the Central Valley
Five years in a roomful of cots   and although
Friends send him the *New York Times*
When lights go out
There are a hundred tossing-turning felons
Stronger than he

In the car   famished   you tear open the box
Choose *perfection*   take small bites as you drive
They set you on edge
Behind   the phantom squad car slides into position
Its siren sounds   red lights pulse

At home   you lay paper towels on the kitchen counter
Tumble these out to thaw: *forever...all my heart...*
Open an '08 Neely Pinot
Decant it   let it breathe

Agate Marie

After he finally let her be
She repaired to the raw north coast
To this trailer she's filled stone by stone
With color and light:
Carnelian   bloodstone   green
Saucers full   bowls full   sills

When the sun comes through the window
The calico cat with melted ears—
Cost of once napping in a dryer—
Lies dazzled

While Russ lived
He was king of the mill
She under his knuckle swore:
Dammit   you want me to work all day
Fuck all night
A truckload of grape stakes sold
He'd spirit the money to town
Get drunk and pass out
C-notes in the bars

I could always tell when he'd been drinking gin
See it in his eyes when I opened the door
Right before he hit me

She walks through calcified stumps of ancient trees
To fresh-tossed gravel beds   kneels
The two fingers and half-lopped thumb of her left hand
Guide the rake

At night in the freedom of her bed
She hears the rock tumbler growling on the porch
Thinks of her planter box
filled with four-leaf clover

II

Landlocked

(The Admissions Officer)

You walk in from Ukraine
Strafed eyes and a small pink mouth
Right away I hear a voice   *help her*
Another whisper   *reach to trace her cheek*
Flushed in this crossfire I admit you to school
To glimpse your face in hallways
So each night it will fill with the gaining moon

And I'm walking up that streambed looking for water
And find again cut under a bank   the pool
Where trout lie locked in formation
Held by the rippling flags of their tails

Each day their world warms   shrinks
It's harder to breathe
And while they must be starving
They won't touch my bait
Here on the shaded grass in my fourteenth year
I learn my heart   it is full of boulders and rain

Now that I'm older   rain and dynamite

Suspended above you at your desk
Held by the rhythm of your fingers on the keys
I see down the clear distance between us

Compliment

Before you were born   I searched for you
Wrong country   more than two decades wrong
My tongue polishing the old words:
Translucent   alabaster   symmetry
Then you walked in   moving a little sideways
I didn't see your hands were full of poems
Or what each poem would cost or who would pay
I noticed your frayed cuff   smudge of poverty

When I was a young man   my father said
You have a strange compassion for the weak
The way he said it with such kindness
For years I thought it a compliment

Eye Contact

(The Job Developer)

Eye contact   I tell the class   *is an art*
Five to seven seconds   slide away
Return with fresh attention
Don't be modest and look down
They'll think you have something to hide
Don't stare   and here I find a pretty one
Lock eyes with her until she colors

When is it okay to stare?
There are smiles across the room
When you're in love   yes
You look into one another's eyes
To intoxicate
But no   not in a job interview
Over at the class's edge
Nearest the door in case you must escape
I see you're laughing
If I'm funny   clever   it's all for you

After class I ask you to stay   ask about your mother
Ill after a friend's death
We sit facing   I'm speaking
And gradually aware
Your dark large eyes are steady to my eyes
They stay   I speak   impossible
They stay   I falter   return your gaze
My future begins to tilt

Commute

I could stay home
But begin in darkness
Neighborhoods dark from the outage
Only stoplights flaring red
Say: *Stay off the road*
But I'm out here with other fools
Trying to get south through breaking day
As rain defines the wind   and wind
Sweeps down hills in loops
Cuts horizontal   bullies us out of our lanes
Everyone's scared here
Locked above his steering wheel
As leaves and branches cartwheel past
The top of a family's camper shears off
Crashes the center railing
And *the other guy* hydroplanes   fishtails
Fights to get back straight
All this time   I'm driving with one hand
Writing this: *Rain is rice on the windshield*
Rolling the window down to bite at the storm
To yell: *Throw it   Throw it*
Tempting the pines along a ridgeline
To sway my attention
I even hum with the harp of the Golden Gate Bridge
Until a semi crowds me toward the rail
Then I roll through debris over San Francisco streets

I could have stayed home
But have to see your face
You look up as I enter the classroom
Your eyes sweep past
The coolness of rain

Muir Woods

Now   after five months
You've entered my bones
Sit wrapped in your raincoat
Across from me at *Doidges*
Letting me order your eggs
And the style of your eggs
You talk of your brother's operation
We'll stay strong   I say
Stupid mistake
On our way to the car
We step over branches laid down by the storm

The gate to the park is locked
An understanding ranger lets us in
Today I control my dreams

There are miracles in a closer look
So many trees so gravely burned
Grow strong around their scars
I mention this but don't insist

We wander the narrow path near Redwood Creek

You say nothing   shake your head
Pull the straps of the raincoat tight
Angle your body a few degrees away
A tall   self-conscious   lovely girl
I fear you're fearing what I might do

As rain gathers in high branches
Drops with fat   delicious smacks
Against the umbrella I hold to shield us both
Not to pull you close   although it does

Immigrant

If you moved back to your country
I'd follow   take a room
In the lowest district of Lvov
The worst I can imagine
Begin to learn the rough grammar
Of life cut off from friends   profession
Those who love me
I'd watch my *kopeyki*
But spend too much for a coat
Find restaurant work   be found slow-witted
Let go   have to look again
I'd sleep with roaches   but emerge clean

All this for a warm morning
To sit outside a café
And see three nurses approach along the sidewalk
They are crisp and laughing at something shared
You at their center see me and weave in
Touch my shoulder with your fingers as you pass

What You Missed When You Said No

The scale of the Central Valley
How the land folds into foothills
How Hangtown got its name
The American River chock with snowmelt
Dropping   shelf by shelf   toward us   down the canyon
The sound water makes heard from that bridge
How the magnet in the mountain pulls us up
Where May snow fits against its granite
White on gray like a puzzle
My telling of what the starving Donners did
Long climb to a last corner
Shock of the Tahoe Valley   lake silver on blue
Nearing it shades of blue in blue
Lunch at that restaurant within a moat
Face to face at last   I'm shy from your letter
We're both attracted   curious
Then coming down Highway 89
Gold country   stopping at an overlook
We get out of the car   I say
Look at me
Repeat the words you've written

Himalaya

*—a wild blackberry brought to the U.S. from India
by Luther Burbank*

1

A little high   an inch too far
Two early-ripe berries nod from their vine
I've strayed from the path in T-shirt and shorts
Lean   reach   fail to note
The slope at my feet
Camouflaged by wide green leaves
As I pick the fruit
Begin to fall   slow motion   forward
Fall   cushioned a moment then released   through green
Into gray thorns   a thicket
Of steel teeth   and I'm dead weight in their strict embrace
The cost of escape—
Where any move is punishment—
Catch at their canes to haul myself out

Licking juice and blood from my fingers
I weave down the path
Face   arms   legs crisscrossed with fire

2

Don't do this   she warns
We are driving up Waldo Grade
But I can't hear
Can only see sweet dark eyes
Have the new key in my right front pocket

Razor Moon

How many times will you love in your life?
What are the odds she'll love you?
If the music starts it must be played
I didn't dream it would sound like this

Take a fix on the moon
Quicker than you think and unreliable
Climbing at an angle from the apple tree
Bright as blade

My fingers in your dark   damp hair
Can't get enough of the shape of your skull
You love me   I'm married   I love you
And am old and haven't counted
How many ways it makes a difference
I shouldn't touch you but I do
You lean to me
My mouth moves along your cheek and neck

You ask   *do I hurt you?*
Never before in my life

This slices to bone
I didn't know it would cut like this

Parked Near the Palace of the Legion of Honor

You wait for me to fall into impatience
When I do   the form it takes is a story:
A man fell in love with the statue of Venus de Milo
Trite   but important to tell
Because he left his family
And taking only his sleeping bag
Became a nuisance at the museum
At intervals throughout the day
Guards dragged him to other rooms
He slept in the weather
As near as he could
To her imagined arms   and so on
After a few months
She told him she loved him
All this time back in his village
Real hearts were breaking

I pause   wait for you to say my story's wrong

First a raccoon and then a skunk
Forage toward a garbage can
While past your shoulder   through the glass
At the fountain at the center of the lot
All this time   a couple has been embracing

The Pines of Chateau Chillon

(at the Sausalito apartment)

Management called those pines a nuisance

So   stabilizing lines go on
Saws buzz branches from tip to root
High limbs fall   buoyed   light as fans
Are fed into a chipper   It chokes and clears
The naked pole's now cut
Lowered   sectioned
Chips   needles   twigs swept into bins
Loaded into trucks marked: *Artistry in Trees*

This happens thirty times   then nothing's left
But great pale coins flush against the earth

Now in A-7 we chip and nick
I'm giving it up   moving out
You always threaten but never do
Call tomorrow and see who answers

But I photographed each tree before they took them

Wedding and Aftermath

Shuddering   running on fumes   lost on the road
I'm late to the celebration
Fumble the unwrapped silver serving tray
In the lot
Then   standing   sweating at the rear of the church
Hear their distant vows
As a good friend marries in Christ
A long-sought   longed-for bride

At the reception   singed by all this good will
I move past banquet to open bar
Soon become the boor   serving *one for you and wine for me*
To faint contempt
I absorb each shock   each chilled grenade   with pleasure

Then settle at a table among strangers   a few friends
The stunning day   numbs   gives way
Are you all right?   Is he driving?   Is he okay?
We'd better call his wife

But before she can arrive   the stairs

Where orders from the brain come   anesthetized
Discordant fingers strum banister strings
Body folds   crumples to the bottom

Blood everywhere   a rush to help
Blood on the wedding dress

Pentimento

I saw you again yesterday
Eating breakfast in a restaurant
Across from Molokai
Now you were blonde   impossibly young
Camouflaged as a tourist
And with another man

Funny   in the library   you were old
Lines on your face fine as on antique china

This morning   you were in the tile
Around me in my shower   your face   form
Lost pointillist prints
Coming out of blue-gray panels

Jazz Alfresco

In a crease among hills
Within a darkening meadow
Where a net of black and white cords   gathers—
The sax is her breath along my neck
That long-ago night in the car   whispering—
Here too   bunched brights   poured blue
A drum's controlled scatter
Bone sliding on skin

No one cares that *my heart stood still*
But I'm here
Digging the ache of dog-bite memory out
Digging a note holding long as life

III

Ora and the River

I. Headwaters

First drops   engineered
Trickle through an arrangement of stones
Into a wading pool
Where tourists photograph the kids

It escapes   slips like a canoe
Through alder and pine
Past sand hills   rice beds
Slips colder and colder
For sixty-five river miles   *north*
Until shouldered by a slant of ancient scour
Forced east
Threads through lakes   bends down
To suffer the first dams
Falls by degrees to the town
Named for what it destroyed

What happened to them rapids?
In that picture in the mill
they was crazy wild

Dynamited   gone under in the millpond

The mill hoards the river, but if you were a white man at the
turn of the Twentieth Century, what did you care about lost
energy and roar? You took the mill job. Safer than working in
the woods. And the new sound of the mill, the enormous
rollers and ovens turning pulp into paper? It sounded like
money to you. Only later, in the early Twenties, retired in
town, you'd think way back, how it had been, how the water
sounded. And if you were lucky—if the mill hadn't deafened
you—that roar down its natural three-mile chute came back as
if you were tuning through static across your new radio dial,
found a powerful music; you'd catch it, have it for a while until

it slipped into static again. And when it was gone, that weave of music and applause, you missed it.

Grand Rapids: After the river was dammed and the water rose, the Ojibwe settlements drowned, their sugar trees drowned, and the pit where, in new moccasins, they'd threshed wild rice. The people fled uphill to ledges, to wait for the next move of the Great White Father.

Today above the dam   a pretty lake
Below   a small release is joined
By a cord of treated piss from the paper mill—
When water goes through a mill   you lose hope for it—

This strange tea flows beneath a bridge
Where Ora   a Red Lake Indian on her way out of town
Stands watching near a sign:
MISSISSIPPI RIVER

A few miles down   from the bridge at Jacobson
The water's become a snagged black sludge
Crawling with nightmare creatures

Farther downstream   creeks bathe and feed
The river gains color   green and brown
Becomes for the first time   a companion
There   through silver maple
A single fisherman aims his boat upstream

Still small   a hundred feet across
The river leans into its first meander
(Later meanders pinched off like young bulls' balls
Steers them straight)

What may be a bald eagle
Tacks high above the heat

A feather of dust plumes from Ora's car on the gravel road
Settles in a hyphen of light oil

In front of driveways   of homes
Where barns slump   silos stand

A white-tail deer on the shoulder of the road
Springs stiff-legged away
Black-eyed Susans in fields of sun
Black flies boil in shade
Signs: *The Porky Pine Inn   Broasted _hicken*
Towns she'll never visit   There's a song on the radio:
Tequila Makes Her Clothes Fall Off

By the time she gets to Little Falls
The river she knows   flourishing   wide   light green
Pivots left   where on the western bank
A museum white as bleached femur   honors the pilot
Who flew so far   into the Führer's lap
Wind blows upstream   creates whitecaps
They collapse face down into trenches

Ora says: *If Lindbergh*
Had been governor of Minnesota
There wouldn't be an Indian left

In a small town   mayflies
Forced south by PCBs in Lake Pepin
Slather the panes of Burger King

Bikers here for Catfish Days
Swarm in   helmetless   gray hair flying
Chat gruff in Rudy'z   guzzle LaCrosse   tongue cherry shots
Gaze out at their machines

Ora at a table in the sun
Feels always under suspicion
Rolls an unopened beer
Across her beaded forehead
Then *crack!*   chugs half of it down
Places the can in the shadow of her skull

Her sister's missing
Fled south from one disaster
To be swallowed by another
Erased   no house at the address
Cell phone dead
One earlier call   a strangled giggle

Dark under windshield
Ora drives through Victory
Bands of pressure ratchet her chest
She feels she's facing an operation
Has to walk right in and let the doctors cut

At the landing   a trailer park
Pickups   boat racks   boats
The river here less than a mile wide
Willow bars hard to sort in the green blend   Signs:
Battle Island   Battle Bluff
As though there'd been a war
She stops   gets out   leans to touch
A chipped stone tablet
Her fingers move on raised stained letters
She closes her eyes
Begins to hear faint cries grow loud
As the monument blurs
Dissolves like salt   her hand goes through it

She looks out on a flood plain
Falling gently to the river
Pickups   cars are gone   trailer park   road
Vegetation shifts
Only the river appears the same

II. The Sauk Massacre

1832: Dying of hunger and injuries, the Sauk nation—reduced to a thousand—is desperate at work in the clearing. Women and older children drag small cottonwood logs to teams of raft builders, silently run for more. All but the builders glance uphill: staccato shots from rifles, shouts, smoke drifting above the brush. A brave rolls out of the cover, naked except for loincloth, left arm shattered near the shoulder baring a spear of bone. He gets to his knees screaming, too weak to lift his rifle. Other braves emerge. Through brush, a furious hidden snarl. Exposed warriors tear saddles from horses, lie prone, this leather their only protection.

The Sauk, trying for days to surrender,

The U.S. militia works free of cover, forms two long lines. A few fall from Indian fire. At a captain's command, the front row kneels, aims. They are dressed in once-white pantaloons, ragged, short gray jackets. Most are shoeless, feet bound in muddied clots. Their captain, lanky, ugly and young, lowers his raised sword. *Fire!*

Ora knows him.

are killed under white flags.

In the clearing, old squaws, old men at their pipes, have turned away like livestock from wind-driven hail. They fall, and as they die release the children. Below, at river's edge, boat builders are ripped away; those waiting to board die waiting. The first blood colors the river. Their saddle protection shot away by musket balls, braves break, retreat downhill, pushing, dragging the remaining old and young. The captain raises his sword toward a second volley, but his men, sensing the rout, abandon ranks, surge down *where the meat is.* On the river, an armed steamboat swings into position. The soldiers, yipping, stab and club. Only the Indians' horses that whinny and wheel at their stakes will live. The tribes absorb the shock of musket ball, rifle butt, and lunge of bayonet. A few braves dive into the water, stroke for a river bar. As they swim, the steamboat's cannon sounds. Those not killed disappear into slender willows. Shot rakes the islands. Leaves, twigs fly up. Debris from exposed tree limbs trails under smoke downriver.

Ora sees the blood. It folds into the current, slickens the riverbank.

Why wouldn't the white man understand

Young women begin to strip, enter the water, children on their backs, locked fingers under mothers' chins. Some infants held by their hair in women's teeth. Sharpshooters sink them as they swim. Hundreds now dead; soldiers lunge for women. The men grab their thin wrists, drag them into undergrowth, where in a little while, knives draw across throats or pistol shots sound, and soldiers emerge, fresh snatches of black hair at their belts. Some have long strips of flesh that make *first-rate razor strops*. One, in ecstasy, presses a young girl's scalp against his crotch.

...white flags?

One woman uses buckskin strips from the fringe of her dress to tie her baby to a curve of cottonwood bark. Pushed out, the little boat spins, returns to shore at an officer's feet.

All afternoon, bodies float downstream, poled into the current by a clean-up crew.

And Ora knows he was there
That man she sees every day
In copper and paper and stone

III. The Upper Mississippi

The Army Corps of Engineers has sliced, cleated and bloused the river.
Billions of dollars arrive from Congress. Concrete flows.

Rain feathers in across the river's face
Darkens the outer walls of a thirty-dollar cabin
Where Ora pokes through a tin
As though choosing a button or mint
Takes two white tablets
Soon the pain descends by steps
Toward a cool cellar   and with each level down
A little surrender   a rinse through her brain
A feeling clean as childhood
And the world's all right
If it isn't   if she's addicted   so what?

How else is she to accept that river carnage
Accept she'd abandoned those children she loves
Became a change girl for the penny slots
In the lint of a cheap casino?

From up here
Mark Twain overlooks the river
Its surface shining wide as when he breathed
And even when you know it's an illusion
It still looks mighty—even as Black Hawk fierce in chains
After he'd fled his people.

The river's on display   the statue looks out
Past the eastern shore and the smokestacks
To the patched green beyond   while below
Through a bleached   shuttered Hannibal
Where barefoot Sam fished for his future
Birds flush to the siren
As the cops chase another meth dealer out of town

Out of its final prison locks and dams   the river blinks in the sun
Freed too late   an innocent old felon   free from all hope
Joined by the molded Missouri
Once chock with careering trees and ice chunks
Two rivers now one   sheathed in levees
Slide south

IV. The Lower Mississippi

Ora   driving the giant muddled river—
Now beaten   thoroughly used—
Passes a slumped burial mound
And soon the Delta opens
Cotton fields   roadhouse bars   the river absent
Heat and haze of the blues coming on

In the dark club   Big Jack Johnson   beautiful in sweat
The lights on the head of his guitar
Blinking in sequence—as when folks who've been away too long
Driving at night
Down a hill through trees
See the intermittent lights of their hometown

Then   pockets full of harmonicas
On comes Charlie Musselwhite

All the way downriver
Ora's seen shadows of clouds
Pushed by no prevailing wind
Around displaced blacks up to cold Chicago
Indian women in ragged gowns
Across to Oklahoma
Shadows darken   too   that massacre up at Bad Axe
The burning   drowning men of the Sultana

Under its canopy of alder and oak
The Natchez Trace unspools
Takes Ora southwest   45 miles an hour
She thinks again of her sister   combing her daughter's hair
As she exits to the antebellum South
Ora needs a drink

Down through streets of mansions
To the Lady Luck under the hill   a riverboat casino
Gangplanked and fastened to the shore
Where an old man at the bar

Caresses his unlit meerschaum pipe
Orders whiskey and coke in tandem
And between deep pulls
Tells of a dicey day on the nineteenth-century river:
Twenty infants on a Sunday sunny cruise
A boat that hit a snag and listed sharply
And what the panic did   screaming   fainting mothers
A squall of babies thrown from the upper deck
To plunge like cannonballs into the river
But men had swum to net them as they hit
With basketed hands   let the force of the babies' fall
Continue through the surface   a kind of baptism
And they never lost a one

Now he leans to Ora on his right
When he opens his left hand   she sees
A pock of cigarette scar in its palm
Then looks past him down the bar
To a woman with dark gold hair
And a smoky   corralling   gaze

Ora wakes alone in a four-poster bed
In a sky-blue bedroom of an empty house
Her mouth hurts   she remembers little   but knows
She'd whispered *Yes* ahead of the question
Soon   she'll wander the Quarter   New Orleans
Pulling like petals from a flower:
Laura...Lorna...Madeleine...

Driving down old Route 61
She daydreams she's a privateer
Breaks into the boondoggle office
Of the Army Corps of Engineers up north
Liberates those squirreled billions
Bales of hundred-dollar bills
Pushes off into the current   all the way down past Hannibal
Past Clarksville and St. Louis   dams melting away

She's a speck of green on a muddy flow
Narrowing into meanders   bouldered revetments at every other bend
And the river   shining like a fish in the sun
Slips on down the Delta
Near New Orleans   a crowd of the hopeful cheer from the levees
Docked   she breaks open the bales   pitchforks money off
To local builders   hospitals   schools   to folks in need

Now   Ora senses the river deepen   speed
Drop into Cancer Alley
She lowers the windows to welcome the tropical air
The chemicals

In Café Pontalba at Jackson Square
(Don't let her get started on him)
Under a thickened sky
Coins of rain enrich the flagstones
Wind licks at the dollar bills held down by Ora's beer cup
Here the Caribbean walls are open
There's a bliss of fear down her spine
The wind a shivering whisper of Katrina
Lightning flickers
And thunder breaks around   through her
Under seven brown ceiling fans wobbling at different speeds
She drinks deep
Looks out above frosted   etched panels of Old New Orleans
Through the soft air   slow jazz of Louis' song
As he plays on   St. Peter's tolls: 4 p.m.
Pigeons flurry and flutter back   a couple of them
Trip in for lagniappe and a drink   a waiter brooms them out
Now   the rain releases   she's inside it
Smells wet ash on the wind
In the distance   woodpecker hammers pause

In Hotel Monteleone   a circus scene
Ora drinks Jack Daniels neat
As above the revolving bar

Faces of ravished cherubs in bas relief
Held fast   pouted and knowing under yellow curls
And the bar creeps glacially counterclockwise
Smooth but for tiny jerking   minute release
Dangerous whiskey   dangerous memory:

The biology classroom down the hall
Red Bank High
Weiss   who thought in a prior life
He'd been a Nazi soldier
His murdered grandfather's guns
A ninth-grade class
Ten   including her sister's girl
Lifted like angels through the ceiling
Away from this world of blood-spattered texts
Her sister leaving her car door open
Running toward the school
Her eyes as Ora stopped and held her

And the mouth of the Mississippi
Is a fire hose nozzle out of control
Slowly whipping west
The river   now bruising past half-hearted levees
Will one day take the lure
Of Atchafalaya's steeper gradient
One morning   New Orleans will wake
To a mudflat of flopping fish

But not yet   not while the Mardi Gras Indian
His fingers scarred by years of needle pricks
From sewing life to fantasy
Smooths his purple feathers and emerges
Resplendent   eight feet tall in the predawn chill

Out at the southern verge
Salt water overlaps the protective marsh
A future Katrina borne in the mind
Will strike and the city sink

Not yet   not while out on St. Charles
A song from a second story
Falls over the surging Friday street
Strangers shift   blend into dance
And the sight of a woman's ample ass
Compels a man in the line behind to plead   *Mercy!*

Ora has been here seven months, has a tiny slice of an apartment, a job at Harrah's. She's not found her sister, doesn't know if her lover ever arrived.

Sunday evening, a warm rain blows north. From far away across and to the right, Ora hears sound impossible to identify, high-pitched, low in volume. It's the same as old radio; as darkness begins to close, it's clearer, louder. Ora stands with a woman she's found, left arm around her, between neck and breasts. She pulls her back against her body and kisses the top of the woman's damp head as she might kiss a freshly-showered child. Fiercely now, she wills this to last forever, vows to hold on. Low clouds weave between tall buildings opposite; balloons, wisps of streamers, bits of heaven-knows-what come by, threading the wind. Rain slants in the dark spaces between buildings, and the sound she's been hearing grows louder until she knows what it is. It comes from throats like hers, upstream. The rain, tropical, intensifies. A vanguard of police, high wild roar of the crowd rolls in, now only a block away. There's a great white skull and then the first band marches, marches in place, green and gold energy, swing and glitter of horns. The nearing float—and it does float—grows far larger than life, now to her right, approaching, almost in front. Sound swallows her. Now the float is in front, strange, beautiful, stark in the rain. Masked creatures up there, treasure-draped, dip and fling toward lifted snagging fingers. And then it's past, the sound alters and more bands and floats until beads and plastic pearls are everywhere, hanging from upper branches of trees, lampposts, street signs.

Fat Tuesday: This morning, she can't steady her fork above scrambled eggs. Flustered, she goes out where sunlight on Bourbon Street glances from plastic beads already coming down; blushing women, braless, slide shirts to their necks; alley vendors set their planks, bank ice around numbing beer; Ora buys two; they're so cheap; an eight-foot tall erection passes with its clapping counterpart, men are calling *Hey, baby!* even to her, and she doesn't like it, might go with a woman, but she'd miss this; the day, though it's not yet noon, falling away; and there's Abe Lincoln under his tall silk hat; students with plastic milk jugs, sloshing of white wine; Christian soldiers in formation, their banners, and their scouts spying drunks, in the name of Jesus yanking them, pushing them up against the iron fence in front of St. Peters to force the gospel through darkness; Ora in close quarters feels hands of a cleric, tries to punch at his mask, can't twist her arm high enough; police on horses—worst job in the world today—veteran in a wheelchair, relaxed, urine tube buried in a planter box, guzzling with his friends; she has another icy two, refreshing, bitter; colors mix and separate; music from every direction, and the wail of the Rex parade; combined voices she's never heard; then love at first sight, and they're in Ora's room, but the woman passes out...luxury of a bathroom...Ora's back outside...where's her wallet; oh, in her front pocket, okay... maybe a gin and tonic if she can find a place to sit...heaven to get out of that heat, gin burns good; a cross-dresser sitting splay-legged on steps outside, great tufts of wiry red pubic hair escaping from sensible white panties; she's sorry for all those who never come to this...who'll never discover...adrift in The Chart Room...an old woman in a pink boa on the stool to her left...martini a foot high with an egg of an olive, explains... *In alcohol, we will have our moments*...somewhere a curling saxophone...Ora braids its honey with Maker's Mark...where's her gin?...she wants to be everywhere...wants out of time the way they promise, but isn't, or why would she feel this ache...

exhausted...maybe a nap...maybe she'd still be there...where the hell is it?...what's my address?...just a nap and then back out...tries to get up...legs have lost their bones...jelly-boned, finds the street...bandied by the crowd...sees that stovepipe hat...loses it...spots it again...lurches through...jumps to swipe it off...misses...careens away...lost in the flow.

IV

Desuetude

—West Molokai, 2004

On the evening the Sheraton opened in '64
Attendants   crisp in white jackets
Moved among diners
Lifted hot towels with silver tongs
From wicker baskets

Today   generations of mice
Pile up against the padlocked restaurant wall
While back on a peninsula behind you
Lepers leach away
Last ashes of an ancient fire

On this deck chair sticky with salted filth—
All other recliners at the littered pool bent forward—
You steep in a smell both sour and sweet
Look up where ratty palms
Ache in a hard wind

Rabbits: Laysan Island

Abandoned by a careless sailor
Cast out on this verge of a dash
Little larger than a sand bar
They're driven to shelter by gouging beaks
Hide in scrub in dunes
Where they find abundant grass   multiply
In time   take dominion

But later   there's no more space
Some are crowded into the sea
Where dark shadows gorge

Grasses   bushes   gnawed below the quick
They turn their gentle eyes on one another
Any drop of blood from a scuffle
They're like red-ass   raggedy-ass chickens
Torn apart
This is how they learn to eat their newborn

Timeline

The black mamo   funeral bird
Sooty as a flue   smaller than a human infant's fist
Niched for an inch on the upper slopes
In the forest on Mt. Kamakou
And never saw the end coming
Brooded in its home on the ground
As the first black rat's nuclear teeth
Flashed in the filtered light
Of a tropical moon

Marama at Moa'ula Falls

1

Two jigsaw puzzle whimsies:
You   looking for a small black bird
That disappeared a hundred years ago
Marama   going for a swim
In the pool up under the falls

You start at the bay   a puzzle tab
Snapped blue in a blank in sandy brown
Then follow the river that empties here
Below where it drowns in green
These are the easiest pieces to find and fit

She leads you up a grass-choked road—
Yellowish brown on the lid of the box—
You've dressed her in shorts and halter top
Then added a T-shirt to mask the tattoo:
Angelfish in a net

She's eighteen or any age you choose
And has quite a mouth on her   doesn't she?
Where did that come from?
Like on the trail   when you say
I think I'm becoming Hawaiian
She stops   turns   flows back
Deceptive warmth in her eyes
You wish

In the understory halfway to the falls
You rest on a low rock wall—
One of many seams in the jungle floor—
While she tells of the tropical ice age
How it strewed what you see through the trees
Chunks of unassembled mountains   greens and gray

2

On a limb near the pool   inside the water's roar
You find the bird (how easy)   Marama swims
You'll take their pictures   close your eyes—
A no-more-than-ordinary blink—
Open them   the piece is missing where the bird should be
The part of the pool where she was swimming   gone

Deleting Marama

Washed up here   you look back
Across the channel to the dark island
Where Mt. Kamakou drowses in cloud

She's still there   where you left her

You knew she ached for her father
The one who gave   then took
Sure   after him   she bounced from boy to boy
Got that tattoo
Was working her way through chemicals to ice

One night   police spotted her
Naked and high out on Farrington
Wrapped her in a blanket
Put her in their cruiser
Then took a wrong turn   took the blanket back
Took turns   took their sweet time
Finally took her home

Shearwater fledglings   abandoned in their nests
Have one chance   to fly at night
Dive into the stripe of moonlight on the sea
Some attracted by stadium lights   crash

Marama and her classmates battled dogs for those that lived
Cradled the birds in towels

You'd have stayed with her if you could have
Bridged fiction to fact   built your home
On the slope east of Kaunakakai
To bring her bougainvillea   but finally
Floated through days away

Now   across the channel
You see Halawa Valley
Cut deep in the slant of a mountain
You turn   reach out
Your wife allots the pale wine

What Loneliness Can Do

It can find you in a men's room
Uphill from the phallic shrine on Molokai
Enter   you enter a life   or what it's come to
A red marker arrow to the ceiling
Where cliché begins   descends clockwise
Around and around you on whitewashed brick:
In high school   dreams of available Charlene
Lipstick on white corduroy
Precocity   pattern of no work done
Then reckless escape to the sea
Where quick promotion dulls in alcohol
There's time with a Bible   watery confession

In love he's been romantic   in sex a dog

You turn to follow his drift
To a young woman   her chances sheared
Children appear   are buffeted
There's more drink   a family tossed off

Sex again   whatever moves the blood   until

Finally   here in this room
He finishes down at the urinal:
I'm here every Tuesday at 1 p.m.

All Flesh

There are fruit trees behind the house
Who can resist a crisp apple
Grain of pear along the tongue?
The new owner can   *They're too much trouble*
He'll take black scratches on winter sky
In summer   *Can't give the stuff away*
Raking or putting off raking
Then insects come
And the slow harvest of leaves he hauls to the curb

One August night
Trees yawning in a hot wind
He opens his bedroom window
Falls asleep to the slow thud of falling fruit

Wakes to a drumbeat that accelerates
On a strange street in an unfamiliar city
And dressed in polka dot silk
It's nearing the end of festival
Neon falls in puddles around revelers
Reflects them as shades of gray
One   a third-trimester girl   asks
What positions do you like best?
She and the clown embrace
Kiss past her burden   his cherry nose
All are jostled toward some vague city center
Bozo is losing his grip
The square filling with people from all the streets
A few look up   search for the source
Of a gaining insect buzz

At his appointment   the doctor—
Huge belly pulling him out of plumb
Fingers shaking—had said

Things look good for now
But something's got to get us   right?
If not this   we walk outside
Get hit by a meteor or bus

Death Consoles a Diabetic Who Just Hadn't Listened

Thanks for the invitation   don't get up
Lie back on your recliner
You seem to prefer horizontal
Hate walking   so
Excuse me while I take that
Foot
There now
No hurry about the other one
I'll be back
Later   we'll wheel on over to Dialysis
Hours well spent
We'll tell some jokes   anecdotes
Could catch up on our reading
If only the explosions on the landscape of your eyes
Hadn't lowered the lamp
You know I'd stop those impacts if I could
But these days even I'm computerized

I'll let you in on why I take the feet
It's about supply
Remember how they howled down there?
Why do you think they howled?

I must say I love your hard-working heart
So tired   so not deceived

Jazz

In the night river
Lit only along the shoreline by their headlights
Men in hip waders swing their net frames
A few degrees upstream
Let the current knock them over rocks along the bottom
As the men are good   and if they're lucky
They feel secondary shocks
Time   time   and scoop
In the cold air   a tangle of candlefish writhing
Brilliant   muscular

Jazz, Red Wine, Rain

1

You've been scuffed by the day and need
Music   that when it takes you away
Leaves a trail back home   becomes home
As you enter   it turns on the light

Still life   Cabernet in a glass on a varnished stand
Sloe shimmer as you lift it from its frame
Fills your mouth   soft now
So good you don't want to swallow
As you swallow
The wine folds over the music

The beat's outside   invited in
Becomes a meadow in the room where you lie back
It cushions then grows up around you
Joining the others
All work together
Weave into one

2

As a woman standing behind her daughter's chair
Smoothes across one palm the showered hair
Divides it in three and begins

Ev'ry Day

—for Sarah Vaughn and Billy Eckstine;
After the poem: "Ariana Olisvos: her works & days"
by David Dwyer

Though we're told they joined only in song
She   married to men who bled her
He   with a family
None of this is true
On the day he opened a door
To the power of her voice so like his own
They were engaged   then wed   a consummate duet
Soon   between recording and applause
They slipped through smoke   away
To a cottage on the fantail of an island
Shaped like a strange leaping fish   where

Every day

They awoke to ambrosia
In a kitchen warmed by photos of their sons
Biology said she could never have
They spoke in lyrics
For forty years

Though we've read how in brittle California
She shut off the chemo and went home
And how the butcher cut him down
These too are lies

At the end   on another lapping evening
Dressed as they would have for a show
He carried her down stone steps
To the verge of a bay named *Dixie Maru*
Then from beach chairs tilted to touch
They watched for a while where the sun had been—

Until she tugged his sleeve—a farther paradise

After he'd opened the thermos and filled their cups
She whispered   *You don't have to...*   He said
Hush   what would I do?

It's 1990   their ashes wash in sand at ocean's edge
This is true   the rest is lies

Goodbye Red-Eyed Monkey

Here   in the shack you've built   painted green
To disappear against the shoulder of the mountain—

Shack furnished with wickerwork bits
Recollected from island vacations—

You open that bottle of wine you shared with her   *how long ago?*
Carry the scent of cut apple to the veranda

From the hammock you see weather swing low across the valley
Lightning!   Far mumble of thunder as birds feather in

Life sounds cease   all wait release of rain
Intermittent   then strict as morphine cocoon

From the boat   you'd seen their faces
Lanterns strung on the bridge you passed beneath

They're here now   *Is he smiling?*   You might be
Considering such a bombacaceous life

But are following a stream of rainwater
Down the spine of a broad jungle leaf

And the monkey?   Cheated of embrace   it dances the railing
Glares back at you   then springs to a nodding kapok branch

Acknowledgments

I am most grateful to Ellery Akers, Gerald Fleming, Peter Kunz and Judith Serin for their critical help. I also want to thank the editors of the following magazines for the faith they've shown in publishing these poems:

Barnabe Mountain Review: "Ashes," "Eye Contact"
Bayou: "Ev'ry Day"
Big River Poetry Review: "Incident on the St. Charles Line"
The Café Review: "Rabbits, Laysan Island," "What Loneliness Can Do,"
    "Family Cemetery"
Confrontation: "Goodbye Red-eyed Monkey"
Field: "The Cost of Health Care"
Fourth River Review: "Marama at Moa'ula Falls"
Fugue: "Jazz"
The Hollins Critic: "Timeline"
Hurricane Review: "A Question"
Margie: "Local Lore" "Legacy"
Peregrine: "News from Afghanistan"
Redactions: "...The Most Wonderful Smile in Sonoma County,"
    "Jazz, Red Wine, Rain"
Redivider: "Jazz Alfresco"
Skidrow Penthouse: "Ora and the River"
Tulane Review: "Commute"
Umbrella: "Harpo's Monkey"
Visions International: "Who Knew?"
Worcester Review: "Landlocked"

Cover art, "Jungle," by Agnes Scholiers (rgbstock.com/user/TouTouke); author photo by Ellery Akers; cover and interior book design by Diane Kistner (dkistner@futurecycle.org); Chaparral Pro text and titling

About FutureCycle Press

FutureCycle Press is dedicated to publishing lasting English-language poetry and flash fiction books, chapbooks, and anthologies in both print-on-demand and ebook formats. Founded in 2007 by long-time independent editor/publishers and partners Diane Kistner and Robert S. King, the press incorporated as a nonprofit in 2012. A number of our editors are distinguished poets and authors in their own right, and we have been actively involved in the small press movement going back to the early seventies.

The FutureCycle Poetry Book Prize and honorarium is awarded annually for the best full-length volume of poetry we publish in a calendar year. Introduced in 2013, our Good Works projects are devoted to issues of global significance, with all proceeds donated to a related worthy cause. We are dedicated to giving all authors we publish the care their work deserves, making our catalog of titles the most distinguished it can be, and paying forward any earnings to fund more great books.

We've learned a few things about independent publishing over the years. We've also evolved a unique, resilient publishing model that allows us to focus mainly on vetting and preserving for posterity the most books of exceptional quality without becoming overwhelmed with bookkeeping and mailing, fundraising activities, or taxing editorial and production "bubbles." To find out more about what we are doing, come see us at www.futurecycle.org.

The FutureCycle Poetry Book Prize

All full-length volumes of poetry published by FutureCycle Press in a given calendar year are considered for the annual FutureCycle Poetry Book Prize. This allows us to consider each submission on its own merits, outside of the context of a contest. Too, the judges see the finished book, which will have benefitted from the beautiful book design and strong editorial gloss we are famous for.

The book ranked the best in judging is announced as the prize-winner in the subsequent year. There is no fixed monetary award; instead, the winning poet receives an honorarium of 20% of the total net royalties from all poetry books and chapbooks the press sold online in the year the winning book was published. The winner is also accorded the honor of judging the next year's competition.

26069517R00050

Made in the USA
Charleston, SC
23 January 2014